FRANCE
FROM THE AIR

FRANCE
FROM THE AIR

Photographs by Daniel Philippe
Text by Colette Gouvion

Harry N. Abrams, Inc., Publishers, New York

Translated from the French by Margaret Hickey
Map by Line and Line

Library of Congress Cataloging in Publication Data
Philippe, Daniel.
France from the air.

Translation of: France vue du ciel.
Includes index.
1. France—Description and travel—1975–   —Views.
2. France—Aerial photographs.   I. Gouvion, Colette.
II. Title.
DC2O.P4813   1985   914.4   84–24228
ISBN 0–8109–0936–7

Copyright © 1984 Sté Nlle des Éditions du Chêne, Paris
English translation copyright © 1985 George Weidenfeld & Nicolson Limited
by arrangement with Éditions du Chêne

Published in 1985 by Harry N. Abrams, Incorporated, New York
All rights reserved. No part of the contents of this book may be
reproduced without the written permission of the publishers

Printed in France by Offset-Aubin, Poitiers

INTRODUCTION

'What purity of line, what extraordinary clear vistas!' exclaimed the great French photographer Nadar on seeing the first aerial photographs. 'Everything seems so marvellously and breathtakingly well-ordered!' Altitude has the power to erase everything that is ugly, useless and unnecessary, and so it allows us to rediscover the beauty of the countryside. The textures, relief and features of the landscape take on an abstract beauty akin to that of a fine painting. One is struck next by the variety of scenery. Seen from this perspective, the country becomes a miraculous patchwork which man has made still more diverse: each settlement, whether a minute hamlet or a vast town, has its own personality, derived in part from its natural setting and in part from its colour, shape and the regional style of architecture. It is this synthesis that a bird's-eye view highlights so effectively, lending a new dimension to our vision of France.

Aesthetic considerations apart, aerial photography has also become an essential tool in research and scholarship, offering geographers, engineers, archaeologists and town planners a chance to 'read' the countryside in a much more accurate way than they could before, to make new discoveries and to verify what was previously only known by hypothesis. The land surrenders its secrets and familiar features reveal themselves in a new light. The interpretation of aerial photography, already a science in its own right, will continue to grow in importance with the increasingly sophisticated pictures now being taken by satellite.

The geology and history of the land is dramatically illuminated by aerial photographs, which provide a mass of information about the creation of the earth. The contours of the land, for example, bear witness to the mighty eruptions and convulsions of the earth's crust and to the long process of erosion. From the sky we see ancient France, stripped down to the bare geology of its origins. The oldest parts – the Massif Central, the Massif Armorican and the Vosges – date from the palaezoic era, 500 million years ago, when the principal families of invertebrates and the first vertebrates began to make their appearance. At that time the

Maures and the Esterel mountains in Provence were an integral part of the vast Tyrrhenian continent which occupied the whole western basin of the Mediterranean. Then, during the mesozoic age between 247 and 65 million years ago, the mighty Paris and North Pyrenean basins, the straits of Poitou and the plains of western and eastern France were formed. Molluscs were just beginning to flourish in the seas, mammals were appearing on land and the first birds were taking wing. It was much later, in the tertiary era, dating from 65 to 1.5 million years ago, that the land folded, cracked open and forced up the mighty peaks of the Alps, the Juras and the Pyrenees. Their formation created another upheaval: the Tyrrhenian continent sank and the Maures, the Esterel mountains and Corsica became separated from Africa by the Mediterranean. In the south and east the hercynian *massifs* rose up, and the plains of the north, like those of Beauce and Brie, emerged. It was at this time that mammals and flowering plants began to cross-breed and multiply. The quaternary era saw the finishing touches to the landscape; the great glaciers cooled the climate and completed the shaping of the land, determining its final contours and coastline, the nature of its soils and the courses of its rivers and streams. It was only then that *homo sapiens*, the forefather of Cro-Magnon man, finally appeared.

Our understanding of the history of mankind, too, is deepened by aerial photography. It can help to explain why certain regions have retained particular characteristics or peculiarities and why others have changed under the influence of invaders, or commercial and cultural exchange. The nature of the land is indicated by its colour and vegetation, and the breadth of view makes it easier to see how that is related to the surrounding geophysical features, local architecture and farming. The shape of the fields can tell us much about the type of agriculture: a chessboard with no hedges or borders, where there has been *remembrement* – the gathering of small-holdings into larger units – indicates that industrialised agriculture has taken over from traditional farming. The scarcity or multiplicity of channels of communication – paths, roads, canals, bridges, stations and aerodromes – is an excellent indicator of a regional economy. And the outlines and layouts of villages and towns tell of the stages in their development and suggest the nature of the political powers which have held sway over the centuries.

Provence – Côte d'Azur

The photographs that follow take us on a circular journey around the borders and coasts of France, and then north through the centre of the country to Paris. Our exploration begins in the mountains of Provence, just behind the Côte d'Azur, an area of savage, almost violent beauty (*see pages 24–45*). Between the Pyrenees and the Alps lie a chaotic mass of mountains: the Maures and Esterel ranges, and the smaller hills of the Alpilles, Lubéron, Estaque, Étoile, Sainte-Victoire and Sainte-Baume. The colours of the rock – red porphyry, limestone, schist and granite – are magnificent under the burning blue sky, but the area is three-quarters arid due to the poor soil, the dry climate and the *mistral* and *tramontane*, strong winds which sweep over the barren slopes. Forests are rare and fir-trees quickly give way to *maquis*, scrub deliciously scented with wild thyme, rosemary and lavender. The coast under the Maures is rocky, with scree slopes broken by deep ravines, headlands and natural harbours. Through the rocky mountains winds the River Rhône, eventually completing its erratic course at the great delta and marshes that break the southern coastline. The naturally fertile country along its banks has long been a prosperous agricultural area, but in most other parts of Provence irrigation preceded cultivation. Now, however, the region is known for its wheat, olive trees, vines, flowers, fruit and *primeurs*, or early vegetables.

With the arrival of tourism at the end of the nineteenth century – the Côte d'Azur was launched in 1888 – the heat, dryness and spectacular cliffs of crystalline rock that had previously worked against the region's prosperity became assets, and since then the whole coastline has gradually become one massive leisure complex. Each of the *départements* making up Provence has its own attractions. The Alpes-de-Haute-Provence boasts the spectacular Gorges du Verdon and nature reserves at Queyras and Luberon, while the valleys of the Hautes-Alpes have the highest town and village in Europe – Briançon and Saint-Véran – and a superb national park at Écrins. In the Alpes-Maritimes a string of famous resorts back on to wonderful inland scenery; in the Bouches-du-Rhône we find the Camargue, the cultural centre of Aix-en-Provence and Marseilles, a major industrial and commercial port. In Vaucluse there are fine Roman ruins, and the medieval papal palace of Avignon. And finally there are the lovely fishing ports and resorts of Var.

Rhône valley	Between the Mediterranean and the Alps runs the natural corridor of the River Rhône, its scenery a series of wonderfully varied landscapes (*see pages 25, 29, 40–7*). At the southern end of the valley, the river crosses plains rich with vines and fruit trees, but also narrows in a series of spectacular gorges: Donzère, Cruas, Tournon, Tain and Vienne. On either side of the fertile valley are the mountains, sometimes gently sloping and thickly wooded and at other times bare with superb ravines, like those of the Ardèche. Lyons, the capital of the Gauls, grew up where the channels of communication met at the centre of the valley. Famed for its gastronomy and as a city of learning, it is now a major industrial, financial and commercial centre, and the third largest town in France. North of Lyons are the plateaus of the Dombes and the Bas-Dauphiné, once unhealthy areas of swamp and now covered by wheatfields and grasslands, interspersed with large stretches of woodland.
Alps and Juras	Along the eastern side of the Rhône valley lie the Alps and, to the north, the Juras (*see pages 48–53*). Geologists still disagree about the formation of these enormous peaks, but there is a general consensus that without later erosion they would now rival the summits of the Himalayas. The scenery here is spectacular and the geography embraces a great variety of land forms: little plains, narrow gorges, lakes, plateaus, gentle and steep slopes, mountain pastures and impregnable mountain peaks covered with snows that never melt. The southern Alps, which belong administratively to the Provence-Côte d'Azur region, are made up of the untidy Préalpes, which are cut by the valley of the River Durance, crystalline *massifs*, and the Grandes Alpes of the Parpaillon *massif*. They have a dry Mediterranean climate and until this century, when irrigation and domestic electricity supplies were introduced, were very poor. More recently, the economy has received another boost from the advent and huge popularity of winter sports. The northern Alps, which correspond to the old provinces of Savoy and Dauphiné and are more heavily populated, can be divided into very clearly defined zones: the six *massifs* of the Préalpes (Chablais, Bornes or Genevois, Bauges, Grande Chartreuse, Vercors and Dévoluy), the central crystalline ranges (the Aiguilles Rouges, Grandes Rousses, Oisans, and Mont Blanc and Beaufort *massifs*) and, finally, the Grandes

Alpes. Between these peaks snakes the Alpine fault, its course following the Rivers Arly, Isère and Drac as they wind through the mountains. The lower slopes – both the *adret*, or slope facing the sun, which is always more luxuriant than the *ubac*, or slope in the shade – are intensively farmed, the land being divided between fruit trees, wheatfields and even vineyards. Above is a layer of deciduous forest, then pines and fir-trees, and above them alpine cattle pastures with lush grass and marvellous wild flowers. Finally, the snowy mountain tops jut up above the treeline and uppermost rocky slopes. The economy of this northern part of the mountains changed dramatically with the introduction of hydro-electric power during the industrial revolution and, like the southern Alps, it has developed even more rapidly since the arrival of tourism. Visitors are drawn here not only by the winter sports resorts, but also by the famous thermal springs of Évian and Aix-les-Bains, and the great mountaineering centres at Chamonix and in the Oisans basin. Nonetheless, the mountains also remain a paradise for those who seek solitude. It is still possible to find villages with authentic chalets and real Savoyard cafés with wooden bars where you can drink the local white wine, and in the Parc de la Vanoise, an enormous nature reserve high in the mountains, gentians, columbines, spring anemones and edelweiss grow in profusion, while ibex, hazel grouse, capercaillies, marmots, badgers and foxes roam in peace, sheltered from hunters' paths.

The Juras are far lower than the Alps, but less easy to cross. On the French side, the highest peaks are the Crêt de la Neige and the Crêt d'Eau, which lie in the eastern Juras; to the west lie a second series of peaks which reach only 1500 metres. The mountains here have a characteristic silhouette of towering crests, in some places hollowed out by a *ruz*, or anticlinal valley, in others worn by a river into a *cluse*, or transverse cut across parallel folds of the range. The landscape of the high, wide central plateaus of limestone and clay is infinitely varied, and where they drop away to the plains there are rivers and waterfalls, grottos and lakes, forests and expanses of grassy meadow. Once dependent on timber and dairy farming, with vineyards on the sunnier slopes, the area has kept its traditional industries alongside more modern enterprises. However, the towns, often sited at the mouths of the long enclosed valleys, are still small, and the superb, sombre landscape remains largely unspoilt.

Burgundy To the west of the Juras lies Burgundy (*see pages 54–67*), once a powerful duchy, its dukes ruling over lands stretching from the North Sea to the Swiss cantons. No one part of the terrain resembles another here: to the east are the mountains of the Charolais and Mâconnais, to the west the Morvan *massif* and, running under the Alps and the Juras, the plain of the River Saône. The plateaus sloping down to the River Saône between Mâcon and Dijon have been one of the great French wine-growing regions since Roman times. There are now three important areas: the Côte d'Or, stretching from Dijon to Chagny, its prestigious vineyards including Gevrey-Chambertin, Vougeot, Pommard, Corton, Montrachet and Meursault; the second area, the slopes around Chalon-sur-Saône, which produce Mercurey and Givrey, both excellent white wines; finally, furthest south, the Côte Mâconnaise, with less well-known vineyards but still very good white wines. To these must be added the delicious dry white wines of the Auxerrois and Tonnerrois, notably Chablis, and the popular wines of Beaujolais. Alongside its reputation for good living, Burgundy has preserved its rich cultural heritage. The Benedictine abbey at Cluny was in the eleventh century the intellectual centre of Christendom and many of the medieval buildings here are marvels of the Burgundian Romanesque style of architecture.

Vosges Turning north-east from Dijon, we return to the mountains. The Vosges, which extend north from the Juras, have the harshest winter conditions to be found anywhere in France, with scenery of surprising grandeur (*see pages 70–1 and 78–9*). To the south are the crystalline Vosges, running from Alsace to Climont. Here erosion has brought the oldest rock to the surface and where glaciers have hollowed out corries, deep valleys with lakes have formed. To the north are the lower sandstone Vosges, with impregnable rocks and chaotic scree slopes like those of Mont Sainte-Odile. Over half this *département* is still covered with forest, and since medieval times timber has been one of the mainstays of the region's economy. Despite poor communications and relatively little urban development (Épinal, the largest town, has only 54,000 inhabitants), this area is not under-populated, but it is predominantly rural with small scattered communities known as *écarts*. Dairy farming and the traditional linen and cotton industries of the region are still important today. More recently tourism has also become a major source of income: the Route des Crêtes (laid out during the First World War) is now a well-known scenic route, spa towns like Plombières, Bains-les-Bains and Vittel offer health cures, and the downhill and cross-country skiing is the most easily accessible of any for Parisians.

Alsace and Lorraine   When Louis xiv took possession of Alsace at the end of the Thirty Years' War, its beauty led him to exclaim, 'What a wonderful garden!' Made up of only two *départements*, the Haut-Rhin and the Bas-Rhin, it forms a long corridor between the Vosges mountains and the River Rhine. The lovely Alsatian plain with its wide, deep river, prairies, woods, wheatfields, orchards and gentle terraced slopes, imperceptibly merging into the blue mountains beyond (*see pages 72–7*), has seen many changes since the seventeenth century, above all those accompanying industrialisation, but the landscape, towns and villages have preserved the subtle harmony, garden quality and regional characteristics which so enchanted Louis xiv. Screened by the Vosges, Alsace enjoys a much brighter, drier climate than most of north-eastern France, and on the limestone and sandstone hills immediately under the Vosges there are fine vineyards. A famous *route de vin* runs between Ribeauvillé and Riquewihr, Turckheim and Kaysersberg, and it is possible to stop at vineyards along the way to taste the local Riesling and Traminer wines. To the north lies a strip of terraced land on which wheat, barley, hops, vegetables, fruit trees and even tobacco are grown. Finally, there is the Ried, an alluvial plain which was once marshy, but has now been drained and turned into good arable land in many places. The villages of Alsace are small but numerous: full of flowers, cobbled squares with fountains and houses with sloping roofs, dovecotes and lovingly carved wooden shutters, they are so picturesque that it is easy to doubt their authenticity. Strasbourg and Colmar, the most notable towns of the region, are both beautiful cities. Strasbourg, with its magnificent cathedral and old town overlooking the River Ill, is the capital of the Bas-Rhin, while Colmar, capital of the Haut-Rhin and situated much closer to the Vosges, has a pleasingly untidy air and gabled houses above still waters, reminiscent of Bruges or Amsterdam.

A natural access point, and therefore frequently an invasion route, Lorraine links north-western to Mediterranean France and the Paris basin to central Europe. Its distinctive character is the result both of its geography and chequered history; the fertile meadows and lovely valleys have often been little more than a battleground torn apart by fighting and government by force, and the people of Lorraine are stubbornly determined to preserve their traditions and liberty. The climate is central European, with freezing winters and baking summers, and the region's waterways run, not to the western coasts but to the North Sea, via the Rivers Moselle, Rhine and Meuse. There is also a slightly Mediterranean air to the landscape and architecture, with flat-roofed houses reminiscent of Provence. Lorraine has always had the resources to achieve a quiet prosperity: once a great wine-growing area, the slopes of the Rivers Meuse and Moselle still yield quantities of delicious Vin Gris, while to the north of the Moselle valley iron deposits are interspersed with beautiful forests. Beyond Rombas, Hayange and Thionville, strongholds of the iron and steel industry, one returns to lush plains and rolling fields crossed by roads lined by fruit trees. The regional capital, Nancy, is a fine example of French eighteenth-century architecture.

Ardennes

The hills of the Ardennes, to the north-west of Lorraine, straddle the border between Belgium and France. The schist and sandstone plateau is covered with forests and moorland into which the River Meuse and its tributaries have cut deep valleys (*see pages 80–5*), and the lowlands to the south have long been an important access route to Belgium and the North Sea. Industry, capitalising on this favourable position, far outweighs agriculture in importance and dominates the landscape of the Meuse valley. Sadly, many people pass through the area without realising that there are also lovely old forests, dark and deep, full of wild deer and boar, that have remained unchanged for centuries.

Northern plains

The vast space of the northern plains beyond the Ardennes stretches east to Cap Gris-Nez through Thiérache, Hainaut, Cambrésis, Flandre, Artois, Boulonnais and Picardy. This is a sober region with rich land, criss-crossed by orderly rivers, with few natural defences (*see pages 86–91*). Since the Middle Ages, these plains often seem to have been little more than an invasion or trading route, yet at the same time the north has always had the most advanced intensive farming. As long ago as 1701, the king's steward noted that there was more land under the plough here than anywhere else in France, today the north still leads the way in industrialised farming and animal husbandry, with record yields. Picardy gives the impression of an immense field stretching to Artois, planted alternately with wheat and sugar beet. Even the marshy valleys, once wild stretches of land left to the hunters and fishermen, have been drained by a grid of canals and reclaimed for cultivation. In the Somme valley, they have been divided into small market gardens, the only ones of their kind in the world. Many new towns have sprung up this century as a result of the continuing agricultural development, and every road, railway or canal junction is now the site of a town or urban area. Abbeville, La Fère and Amiens, for example, all grew up in this way. However, northern France is now associated first and foremost with industry; during the 1960s it was the centre of the French coal and textile industries. It also has flourishing cement, chemical and metallurgical works, paper mills, cardboard factories, potteries and food-processing plants, and it is the region's densely populated industrial towns and ports – Valenciennes, Douai, Dunkerque, Boulogne and Lille, the region's capital – that provide the spur to continuing agricultural development. Since the estuary of the Somme silted up and port activity on the coast there came to a halt, the coast of Picardy and the Côte d'Opale have become tourist areas, with resorts like Le Touquet, Berck-Plage, Le Crotoy and Saint-Valéry. Here the reaches of sand and marshland have preserved an apparently changeless peace and quiet.

Normandy

Beyond Picardy, on the north-west coast, are the green fields and apple trees of Normandy (*see pages 92–5*). In fact, there are two Normandies: eastern, or Upper Normandy, and western, or Lower Normandy, with the River Seine, the region's main channel of communication, as the dividing line between the two areas. The rich alluvial plateaus of Upper Normandy – the fertile lands of Bray, Vexin and the Pays de Caux – bear a strong resemblance to neighbouring Picardy, and here farming is almost equally divided between cattle pasture and ploughed fields. Inland the houses are scattered and the towns are small, serving mainly as market places for the farmers. Along the coast are towering white cliffs sculpted by the wind and the waves into pillars and spectacular pointed arches, while to the south the River Seine has hollowed out large meanders in the chalk plateaus, and wide plains have been formed by the silt the river deposits as it lazily reaches the end of its course. The suspension bridge at Tancarville – the longest in France – forms part of an important industrial route running through Rouen (the fourth largest port in France) and Le Havre, the commercial and industrial centre and capital of the region.

Lower Normandy is renowned for the greenness of its countryside: the woods and prairies of the Pays d'Auge with herds of cattle and a thriving dairy industry, the limestone country around Caen, Argentan and Alençon given over to the cultivation of cereals, the prosperous dairy-farming area of Cotentin and, finally, the hilly Norman *bocage*, little fields and meadows divided by banked-up hedges. On this section of the coast lie the naval port of Cherbourg, the historic town of Caen and a number of seaside resorts, the most famous of which is Deauville. But the jewel of the shoreline is undoubtedly the abbey and rocky islet of Mont-Saint-Michel.

Brittany

Across the River Couesnon is Brittany, a diverse mosaic of landscapes, each of which has its own distinct personality (*see pages 96–105*). To the north are the Arrée mountains, the moors of Méné and the Norman hills; and to the south the Montagne Noire and the Lanvaux *landes*, which enclose the Rohan plateau and the Châteaulin and Rennes basins. Between these two areas, central Brittany is made up of alternating plateaus and plains. But there is another, more poetic way of dividing Brittany – into Arvor, the land of the sea, and Argoat, the land of woods. Arvor is a region of stunning beauty where the rocks and cliffs, like the Pointe du Raz and the Baie des Trépassés, have a wild grandeur and seem steeped in mysticism. Here dreaming moors alternate with blue-grey granite villages and the ragged coast is scattered with reefs lashed by winds from the north-west and south-east. Yet there is also a more gentle landscape, long stretches of white sand and little islands covered with yellow mimosa. Arvor draws its livelihood almost entirely from the sea. Nearly every bay between the headlands and granite outcrops has a fishing port, and sometimes also canneries or shipyards. The sea even provides the fertiliser, seaweed, which is used to enrich the soil between the Marais de Dol and Cornouaille, and around Quimper, where early spring vegetables flourish in the mild climate.

Argoat, stretching between Rennes and the English Channel, is a long, undulating area of forest, river and heathland with splashes of gold and mauve broom, furze and flowering heather. One of the forests, Paimpont, is better known as the Forest of Brocéliande which appears in the saga of the Round Table and the search for the Holy Grail. Argoat may be divided into two areas: Lower Brittany, furthest west, which is a rather poor area of scattered hamlets and small-holdings where old traditions and the Breton language still thrive, and Upper Brittany, to the east, which is more prosperous. Here the land is farmed in larger units which enables it to be more intensively cultivated, and the area's proximity to the Paris basin has also encouraged industrial development. The land around Nantes is still part of Brittany, although it owes everything to the River Loire, which here widens out into a vast estuary. On one bank is the Brière, a regional park composed of marshy bogland, formerly a source of peat, which now serves as grazing pastures; on the other the Retz plateau surrounds the lake of Grandlieu. Spring vegetables and muscadet grapes grow on the fertile river plain, while on the coast, there are a series of superb beaches and the shimmering salt marshes of the Guérande. In the seventeenth and eighteenth centuries, Nantes was one of the foremost French ports in the West Indies trade, and it has many splendid mansions built for the wealthy slave traders. Today, the port is not as accessible as it used to be, but Nantes is still the regional capital and a flourishing industrial centre.

Loire Valley Inland from Nantes lies the pale, gentle valley of the River Loire (*see pages 106–13*), described by the French historian Jules Michelet as 'a rough, homespun robe fringed with gold'. This is the garden of France and the birthplace of the *langue d'oïl*, the source of the dialects of northern France. Up to the sixteenth century, the regions of Touraine, Anjou, Orléanais, Maine and Blésois were the seat of French political power, but now only the magnificent châteaus are left to mark their former glory: Chenonceaux, Chambord, Azay and Blois, to name just a few. Some are constructed in such a way that one can perceive a subtle play of pure geometry and perspective; others tell the story of successive stages of building over the centuries. Usually one sees only the façades, architectural details and segments of the châteaus, but aerial photography reveals the overall concept of the layout, the harmony of line and the way in which the gardens and parks were designed to enhance the buildings. The climate of the Loire valley is mild and everything grows in the rich soil: vegetables, cereals, fruit, flowers and vines, which produce the excellent wines of Vouvray, Bourgueil, Chinon and Saumur. Returning to the coast south of the River Loire, we reach the Vendée: *bocage*, or little fields and meadows divided by hedges, then open countryside of arable fields and grazing land stretching out to Poitou. Here the coast is edged with sand dunes and salt marshes, which have been transformed into polders. Delightful little villages are perched on small islands of limestone and canals take the place of roads. Although the coast is not suitable for fishing, or for ports and harbours, its sandy beaches, dunes and healthy climate draw many summertime visitors. Yet even at the height of the season, the region keeps its air of tranquility and spaciousness.

Aquitaine basin

Travelling south through the Aquitaine basin on the west coat, the distinctive landscapes of Charentes, Aquitaine and the Landes (*see pages 114–23*) follow one another. Charentes is bordered by the Côte de Lumière, known for its sparkling light, and has two lovely offshore islands, the Île de Ré and wooded Île d'Oléron, which face the region's largest town, La Rochelle. Inland there are dairy farms, fields of cereals and vineyards, where *pineau*, the famous local wine-and-brandy aperitif, is made. Aquitaine, known as the Côte de Beauté, runs down as far as the Gironde estuary; it has a very mild, almost Mediterranean climate, and beaches sheltered by holm-oaks and fir-trees. Royan, at the mouth of the estuary, is more susceptible to the moods of the sea, which can sometimes be very rough. The long run of sands is carved open by the deep Garonne estuary, which lies in a strip of very fertile agricultural land. Bordeaux, the capital of Aquitaine, is the centre of a great wine-growing area and its long-standing prosperity is displayed by the châteaus (there are well over a thousand) of the surrounding countryside. Many of them control famous vineyards, with familiar names such as Château Larose, Château Lafite, Château Latour, Château Margot, Saint-Estèphe and Saint-Émilion. South of the Garonne estuary are the pine forests of the Landes, the calm waters and famous oyster-beds of the Arcachon basin and, between the Pointe du Grave and River Adour, which rises in the Pyrenees, infinite stretches of white sand meeting the breakers and long swell of the Atlantic. Formerly this plain was nothing but waterlogged sand lying on impermeable bedrock, but since the nineteenth century the landscape, climate and economy have been transformed by drainage and afforestation.

Pyrenees At the edge of the Landes, the profile of the land rises again towards the foothills of the Pyrenees, their splendid peaks forming a natural frontier between France and Spain (*see pages 124–5*). Travel across the mountains is difficult. There are no major *massifs* or longitudinal valleys here, as there are in the Alps, and the perpendicular valleys allowing access to the interior rapidly grow narrow, culminating in lofty summits or high cols. As a result, the people of the Pyrenees have always lived in a relatively closed world, and the pattern of contact today still follows that established by the tiny medieval feudal states, each of which comprised a mountainous area, with pastures, and agricultural land in the valley. The western Pyrenees, bordering Béarn and the Basque country, are the lowest hills and have the least rainfall, but they have good, fertile land and farming flourishes here alongside the industry and lively maritime ports of Bayonne and Saint-Jean-de-Luz. Tourism also plays an important part in the economy, although the local people, many of them Gascon or Basque in origin, are stubbornly independent and resist outside influences. In the central Haut-Pyrénées, between the cols of Puymorens and Somport, are the tallest peaks of the mountain chain. Farming here still follows the traditional rural pattern established centuries ago, with cattle and sheep on the high mountain slopes and pastures, and the cultivation of wheat, maize and vines in the valleys. The installation of hydro-electric power stations and the work created by the tourist trade have arrested depopulation and made the Haut-Pyrénées a relatively wealthy area. Further south, in the Ariège, where natural resources are not so good, the old craft-based industries are dying out, and the valleys of Andorra depend instead on farming, tourism and their tax-free status. Finally, there are the mountains of the eastern Pyrenees, running from the col of Puymorens to the Mediterranean coast. They are tall and grandiose, with a cold, dry beauty; life here is hard, and it is only by continual hard work in the arid fields that the drought and vicious winds can be overcome.

Descending again towards the Mediterranean, the ochre mountains suddenly give way to the orchards and vineyards of Roussillon, and the rich green and red landscape of French Catalonia stands out against a violet-blue sky (*see pages 130–1*). Throughout this region there are marvellous churches and abbeys built in the Catalan Romanesque style, and its towns are as colourful as its landscape: Perpignan, the capital, has the air of an African city, Collioure is Catalan in character, and Banyuls and Rivesaltes, which produce sweet muscat wines, are full of atmosphere. In lower Languedoc, vines stretch as far as the eye can see, and as one reaches Sète and Montpellier, the harsh accents of the Pays d'Oc give way to the lilting tones found east of the River Rhône.

Massif Central Turning inland to travel northwards through the centre of France, we come to the well-named Massif Central (*see pages 132–5*), bounded to the west by Poitou, to the east by the Lyonnais slopes and industrial lowlands of Saint-Étienne, and to the north by the Bourbonnais plateaus sloping gently down towards the southern Paris basin. The waters of the Massif Central feed rivers which flow through an enormous area of France: the Rivers Garonne, Dordogne, Rhône, Hérault, Loire and even, by way of the Yonne, the Seine. Coming from the south, one reaches first the Cévennes, granite mountains streaked with rushing torrents, and the *départements* of Lozère and Gard which, despite the advent of tourism, are still among the poorest parts of France. To the west, facing Languedoc and Aquitaine, are the Causses, where Mediterranean *garrigues*, or hill country, alternate with lush green valleys. Quercy, Dordogne and Périgord share superb *cuisine* and lovely regional architecture, at Toulouse and Carcassonne, for example; here also are the famous cave paintings of Lascaux. The Massif Central has a very different face on its eastern side: the rich slopes of the Beaujolais hills. But the beauty and character of the landscape is most distinctive at the heart of the region, in the Aubrac, Auvergne, Margeride, Gévaudan and Velay. The lakes, shadowy forests, townships built high on the hilltops and volcanic cones, with their bare craters and grassy slopes, give the landscape a profile which is sometimes rounded and at other times sharp and angular. Although the volcanos are now extinct, the smell of sulphur still hangs over the black, green and blue countryside. Small villages cling tenaciously to rocky bluffs while the larger towns, some with thermal springs, nestle in the valleys below. The region is agriculturally poor, reliant on the fertile pockets of land around Puy and Limagne, and the cattle-rearing of the Cantal. Winter migration to the towns began in the nineteenth century and today emigration to other areas of France is very high, but many people still return here to end their lives where they were born.

Paris basin To the north of the Bourbonnais plateaus is the immense area of the Paris basin, the largest natural region in France, covering a quarter of the country (*see pages 136–53*). The plains of Beauce and Brie and the Île de France with its deep green forests and rivers form a ring of fertile land around the suburbs and city centre of Paris. Above the wheatfields of the Beauce the spires of Chartres 'soar up with a purity of spirit and harmony of line' as the poet and philosopher Charles Péguy described it. But any portrait of France must end in Paris, the heart of the country. The city grew up at the meeting point of three great navigable waterways: the Seine, the Oise and the Marne. The site was ideal, with the surrounding countryside providing everything necessary for construction – wood, stone, millstone grit and gypsum – and the hills of Montmartre and Sainte-Geneviève serving as look-out posts. Settlement began on the Île de la Cité, but even in Roman times the town spilled over on to the left bank of the Seine, and soon the marshes on the right bank were drained and in their turn inhabited. Uniquely among river cities, Paris has from that point onwards developed systematically on both sides of the waterway. In the Middle Ages, the city was in a perpetual state of construction, but then the growth of the city shifted to the right bank, where wide open spaces, detached large buildings and long avenues (the Louvres, Tuileries, rue de Rivoli and Champs-Élysées, for example) replaced the labyrinth of tangled alleys and huddle of roofs that can still be found in the oldest quarter of Paris, on the left bank. Until the seventeenth century the city continued to grow along the same pattern; the marvellous proportions and splendid buildings of the Place Vendôme, Place des Victoires and Place des Vosges, then known as the Place Royale, give an indication of its magnificence at that time. In the seventeenth century Louis xiv moved to Versailles, society moved out to Saint-Germain, where long straight roads, parks and mansions were carefully laid out, and new residential quarters took shape to the west, around Parc Monceau and the Bois de Boulogne. The skyline today is also marked by the great nineteenth-century constructions – railway stations, exhibition halls, and, of course, the famous Eiffel Tower – and more recent additions such as the controversial Beaubourg.

With Paris we complete our portrait of France. The magnificent aerial photographs that follow take us on a journey of rediscovery that allows us to share the early balloonists' and aviators' magical experience of gazing down on France from the air.

Chantilly, Île-de-France

Vence, Alpes-Maritimes

As the winding hill road climbs towards Vence (*left*) the noise and bustle of the Côte d'Azur gradually die away until there are only chirping crickets and bees to disturb the blue silence of the Alpes-Maritimes. At the centre of the town lies the original medieval village, perched high in the hills away from surprise attacks by raiders, the pink and ochre tiled roofs of the closely packed houses forming a haphazard spiral around the Romanesque cathedral, the oldest parts of which date back to the beginning of the eleventh century. The cathedral bell rings out the hours in the calm of the day and some traces of the fortifications once encircling the whole village still remain. In this century, pottery, weaving and tourism constitute the most important local industries. But the town is most famous for the group of artists who earlier this century fell in love with the town and made their home here: Matisse, Picasso, Miró and Rouault. Each has left their mark: the Chapel of the Rosary in the cathedral was decorated by Matisse and there are stained glass windows by Rouault, while Picasso and Miró both worked in the potteries.

Arles, Bouches-du-Rhône

Arles (*above*), a lovely city lying on the edge of the Camargue in the Bouches-du-Rhône, takes the visitor still further back in time. The magnificent classical ruins here include a theatre and amphitheatre, the Roman baths and viaduct, and the garden of Alyscamps, famous from Roman until medieval times as a pagan and then Christian burial ground. Between Easter and the grape harvest, crowds throng the arenas where bullfights have taken the place of the Roman circuses. The city's wealth did not die with the passing of the Roman Empire, and the ancient cathedral church of Saint-Trophime is one of the most marvellous examples of Romanesque Provençal art, while along the banks of the Rhône stand lovely old buildings, such as the priory of the Knights of Malta, which houses the Réattu museum.

Entrevaux, Alpes-de-Haute-Provence
The spectacular town of Entrevaux, which clings to a rocky hill face
high in the valley of the River Var, has remained unchanged since
the eighteenth century. The tiny, closely packed houses, built in tiers,
are enclosed by a triangular wall with three gates and drawbridges,
one of which gives access to the bridge spanning the gorge below. The
cathedral, with its crenellated bell tower, is built into the town walls,
and the château, perched on a peak high above the village it once
guarded, is linked to them by a fortified wall. All around the severe,
warlike little town is rubble, and the air smells of white-hot stone and
wild lavender. On the surrounding slopes of the lower Alps are hard-
won terraces and where the valley widens out cultivation has crept in,
so that it is now only the riverbed that is not exploited.

28

Sisteron, Alpes-de-Haute-Provence

Sisteron (*left*) and Grignan (*below*) capture the two very different faces of Provence: the first a military stronghold set against the spectacular scenery of a rugged landscape in the lower Alps; the second a castle-town built in the shape of an amphitheatre, nestling between meadows and lush orchards in the Rhône valley. Sisteron has always been an important strategic point because the Dauphiné and Provence are linked here by a narrow valley of the River Durance. A stronghold was first established in Roman times to arrest the approach of encroaching hordes of barbarians, and in the Middle Ages the pass was guarded by a castle, probably built on the site of a Roman *oppidum*, the last vestige of which, a Gothic chapel, was destroyed in the Second World War. From the sixteenth to the seventeenth centuries the devastation of war, particularly the religious wars between the Catholics and Huguenots, led to rebuilding and periodic attempts to fortify the town more effectively. The citadel, attributed to Jean Érard, military engineer to Henry IV, which defends the bridge spanning the valley, seems to spring out of the riverbed. Today the fighting is forgotten, but visitors can still walk around its intricate system of steep alleyways and flights of steps, and the harshness of the bare and stony landscape remains.

Grignan, Drôme

Grignan lies in the fragment of the Rhône valley known as the Tricastin, which acts as the gateway to Mediterranean France. Here we find a Romanesque church, a collegiate church dating from the sixteenth century and the most attractive of castles – in part Gothic, and in part Renaissance, but also much restored in the twentieth century. Madame de Sévigné, that charming, garrulous woman of letters, often came to Grignan and finally died here; her spirit can still be felt everywhere in the castle.

Pont du Gard, Gard

A bold and elegant masterpiece, the Pont du Gard was built as part of a Roman aqueduct carrying water from the springs around Uzès to the lovely town of Nîmes, with its temples, baths, arenas and gardens. The engineering and artistic conception of this construction are still astounding: the collossal blocks of stone, some of them weighing six tonnes, were somehow raised as high as 40 metres. The canal, which could carry 20,000 cubic metres of water per day, flowed along the top, while pedestrian traffic moved between the lower arches. The three rows of arches, built one on top of the other, form three bridges, the lower one 22 metres in height, while the six arches of the base, anchored in the riverbed, have a breadth of 142 metres. The patina of time deposited on the old stones and the magnificence of the site are an integral part of the aqueduct's beauty. 'The sight of this simple and noble construction struck me all the more because . . . in the middle of a desert . . . silence and solitude made the object more striking and admiration keener', wrote Jean-Jacques Rousseau in the eighteenth century. Today the Pont du Gard remains as awe-inspiring as ever.

Saint-Tropez, Var

Saint-Tropez and Porquerolles, the largest of the Hyères islands, separated by only a few kilometres of blue water and ochre headlands, could hardly provide a greater contrast. Saint-Tropez (*left*), once a corsair headquarters, and later a tiny independent republic, set up by a Genoese gentleman and governed by its elders, was simply a quiet fishing village drowsing in the shadow of its citadel when the Côte d'Azur first became a fashionable tourist area in the mid-nineteenth century. It emerged from its anonymity at the end of the century, discovered first by Maupassant, then, in rapid succession, by the painter Signac, by Colette, Cocteau and the famous *couturier* Poiret. Finally, towards the end of the 1950s, the smart set from Paris adopted Saint-Tropez as their summer capital and it became the crowded fashionable resort we know today.

Porquerolles, Var

Meanwhile, Porquerolles (*above*), just off the rocky coast of Provence, still slumbers in the exquisite scent of its heather and myrtle. Delightfully isolated, with sheer cliffs and chasms along the northern coast and warm beaches along the southern side of the island, the number of residents has been strictly limited to preserve its marvellous serenity.

Port-Grimaud, Var

Port-Grimaud, in the Gulf of Saint-Tropez, rose out of the sea in the 1960s. The property developers, who were by then running out of dry land on which to build, realised that one solution to their problems was to fill in areas of the coastal strip. Despite energetic and often very sound opposition from the conservationists, marina developments began to appear along the coastline. The architect of Port-Grimaud, François Spoerry, deliberately avoided the heavy concrete and rigidity of larger developments like the controversial Marina-Baie-des-Anges near Nice, and instead used the style of traditional Provençal villages, with shady squares, alleyways and small painted houses roofed with roman tiles, to create a purpose-built lagoon-town for water-sport enthusiasts. Nearly all the houses are on the water and have their own mooring immediately below; bridges give access from one islet or promontory to another, and, like the *vaporetti* of Venice, boats provide public transport across the lagoon. And for summer visitors in search of the past, the pretty old villages on the slopes of the Maures are only a short journey away.

La Grande-Motte, Hérault

La Grande-Motte, which stretches along the flat, sandy coast from Carnon to Grau-du-Roi, next to the Étang d'Or, is easily identified by its pyramidal blocks of flats, built in terraces facing the sun. It is one of a number of seaside resorts built as part of an ambitious project to redevelop the Languedoc coast in the 1960s. The first stages of the project concentrated on making the region a healthier place to live, improving the marshes, introducing afforestation and protecting the coastline as the groundwork for a series of new sea resorts which would give a powerful boost to the local economy and relieve the overpopulated Côte d'Azur. Port-Camargue, Port-Barcarès, Port-Leucate, the new town of Gruissan and la Grande-Motte all came into being in this way. Once the basic facilities had been installed by the government and other authorised bodies, the individual sites were handed over to property developers and architects who were given express instructions to ensure that no resort should resemble its neighbour and that the total effect, while harmonious, would not be monotonous. The purpose and character of the new resorts is clear from their construction: holiday villages, hotels, camping sites and leisure centres are clustered around marinas and harbours with line upon line of yachts and speedboats. While many residents argue that the bold architecture of the new resorts clashes with the landscape and has eclipsed the authentic Languedoc villages, with their ochre-coloured houses, pink roofs and green shutters, they nevertheless recognise the contribution of the resorts to the local economy.

Cannes, Alpes-Maritimes

The Riviera was discovered in the second half of the nineteenth century by wealthy British in search of the sun and high living. Today it is a seamless complex of terraced housing and high-rise resorts, where luxury villas stand alongside palaces, joined later by camping sites and clubs, yet even the excessive development does not disfigure the beauty of the Mediterranean landscape. Along the coast between Cannes and Nice wind three *corniches* – mountain roads – the highest laid down by Napoleon, running past Antibes, Cagnes, Villefranche-sur-Mer, Beaulieu, Monaco, Monte-Carlo and Roquebrune-Cap-Martin. Cannes (*above*) was made fashionable as a resort by an Englishman, Lord Brougham, in the 1850s. Le Suquet, the old town, on the slopes of Mount Chevalier, has kept some of the character of

nineteenth-century Cannes, a small town set against the green outlines of the Esterel mountains and the magnificent blue waters of the Mediterranean. But since then Cannes has grown into one of the smartest and largest Riviera resorts with splendid gardens, an elegant seafront, luxurious residences, pleasure boats at anchor in the harbour, and the *palais des festivals* on la Croisette, where the world of cinema gathers annually for the Cannes Film Festival.

Nice, Alpes-Maritimes
Nice (*top*), a little further east, is the capital of the Côte d'Azur. Along the seafront, behind the narrow beach, runs the Promenade des Anglais – named after the British residents who assumed responsibility for its construction – which is lined with palm trees and a series of grand, old-fashioned hotels that were once private palaces.

Antibes, Alpes-Maritimes
On the other side of the bay lies Antibes (*bottom*), nestling between two indentations in the coastline. A pretty old town enclosed within its ramparts, it has now acquired a certain *chic* among Parisian intellectuals, who prefer the *ambience* to that of Saint-Tropez.

Monte-Carlo, Monaco
In marked contrast, Monte-Carlo (*above*) boldly points its roofs to the sky. It is one of three towns in the independent principality of Monaco, the others being la Condamine and, higher up the mountain-side, the capital, Monaco. In the thirteenth century Monte Carlo was a Genoese fortress, but today its major attraction is the casino.

Overleaf : **Aigues-Mortes, Gard**
The harbour of this fortified medieval town in western Provence founded by St Louis, who twice set out from here on crusades to the Holy Land, subsequently silted up and the town lapsed into a golden melancholy that has endured to the twentieth century.

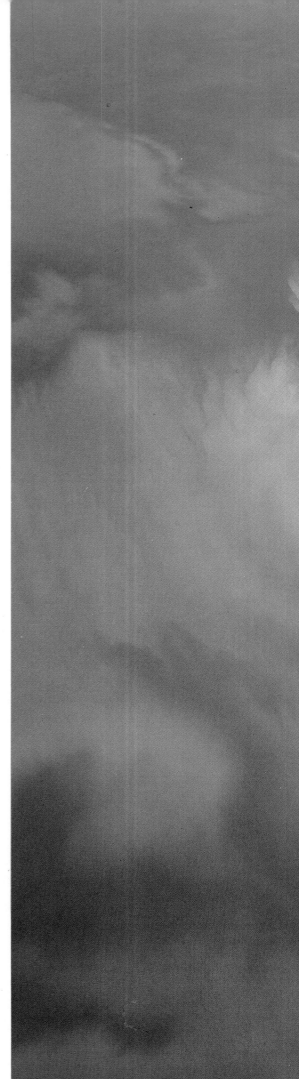

Camargue, Bouches-du-Rhône

The Camargue is a solitary, dreamy place made up of alluvial deposits from the River Rhône, marshes and lagoons separated from one another by alluvial levées. L'Étang de Vic (*right*) is not far from Aigues-Mortes. The ground is steeped in salt and the vegetation turns from green in spring to grey in summer and red in the winter. From time to time, the sea rises and threatens the inland reaches, but the land bordering the principal tributaries of the Rhône has nevertheless been inhabited and cultivated since medieval times. Dykes were built to protect the cultivated fields and pasture used for grazing sheep. Later, in the nineteenth century, the fields were drained, and cereals and vines could be planted. During the Second World War, rice was planted in the salt-marshes for the first time. Today, the Camargue is divided into three zones: the cultivated land that borders the Rhône and its former riverbeds, which is now irrigated by fresh water pumped in from its tributaries; the salination plants to the west of the Petit Rhône and near Salin-de-Giraud, with their network of evaporation basins and *camelles*, little mountains of salt (*below*); and, finally, the nature reserve in the southern part of the delta. This is the Camargue which, with the air of a lost paradise, is known for its herds of cattle and its white horses roaming freely over the marshes, a shelter also for duck, teal, purple herons, white plovers, egrets and pink flamingoes.

Saint-Honorat, Alpes-Maritimes

The abbeys of the Côte d'Azur have managed to remain peaceful oases of contemplation. Two of the most beautiful are the monastery of Saint-Honorat (*left*) in the Îles de Lérins, just off Cannes, and the abbey of Le Thoronet (*below*), in the *département* of the Var. The small, densely forested islands of Sainte-Marguerite and Saint-Honorat, now known as the Îles de Lérins, were settled in the year 400 by the first monks of Western Europe. In 1073, Aldebert, the abbot, had a fortified monastery erected, its defensive walls rising out of the sea on three sides as protection against pirates. There were seven chapels, two of which – the Trinity Chapel of Byzantine inspiration and the octagonal Chapel of Saint-Saviour – still have their ancient façades. Over the centuries the monastery has several times been ruined and abandoned, but each time it has been rebuilt; its inspirational setting – the dense forest of eucalyptuses, cypress and fir trees against the blue of the sea beyond – has remained unchanged.

Le Thoronet, Var

Le Thoronet, crouching between wooded hills at the bottom of a small valley, has preserved the simplicity, humility and purity of the Cistercian spirit. Nothing could be more austere than the church with its humble bell tower, completed around 1190, and the cluster of surrounding abbey buildings and cloisters completed shortly afterwards. Yet there is also a silent majesty about the small settlement that rarely fails to impress visitors today.

Grand-Retour, Vaucluse

Between Valence and Avignon, the slopes running down to the River Rhône take on Mediterranean colours. Here the land is very fertile and arable fields of typically Provençal shape look like boats anchored in a sea of vineyards. The *domaine* of the Grand-Retour (*below*) is typical of the many small estates producing Côtes-du-Rhône wines.

Baronnies, Drôme

Above the Rhône valley, on the slopes of Ventoux, the plateau of the Vaucluse and the Baronnies mountains, cultivation is much more difficult. Here the landscape is a chequerboard of dense green forest and hard-won terraced fields (*right*). The slopes, reaching a height of nearly 2,000 metres, are lashed by fierce winds and covered by snow between December and April, while the temperature can drop by as much as eleven degrees between the foot and summit of the mountains. During the nineteenth century the mountain-sides were stripped of their trees to provide the Toulon shipbuilding industry with the timber it required. Since then, however, all save the highest slopes have gradually been replanted, with holm and white oaks, sea and pitch pines, beeches and larches, Atlas cedars, Aleppo and black Austrian pines, and, as cultivation has developed alongside the forests so the distinctive chequerboard pattern of fields and forest has established itself.

Chamonix, Haute-Savoie

High above the valley of Chamonix, the famous needles of Blaitière and Charmoz-Grépon stab the sky (*left*). For centuries people never ventured on the mountains, revering them from afar as the haunts of demons; then, in 1786, two men from Chamonix, Balmat and Paccard, decided to go and see the peaks. These brave men were the first to conquer Mont Blanc and the first of a long line of climbers. Chamonix has become the capital of mountaineering, a sanctuary for those who want to pursue their passion to climb even at the risk of their lives. But their world exists side by side with that of the skiers gliding down the mountain face, for Chamonix is also one of the most beautiful skiing resorts in France, with the advantage of runs which remain open all the year round.

Courchevel, Savoie

Other famous resorts like Courchevel (*below*), once a simple Savoyard village with the innocent charm of a scene from a Christmas card, are centres of both mountaineering and skiing. For many years Courchevel was to winter what Saint-Tropez was to summer for the Parisian smart set.

Reculée des Planches and cirque du Fer à Cheval, Haute-Savoie

The Reculée des Planches and Fer à Cheval (*right*), a recessed valley and amphitheatre of mountains below Mont Blanc, not far from Samoëns, are open areas of calm. Close by, at Sixt Fer à Cheval, stands a twelfth-century abbey, while at Tenneverge, during the summer, at least thirty waterfalls hurtle down the precipitious mountain-side in a spontaneous and extravagant *son et lumière*.

La Plagne, Savoie

The northern Alps have become a playground, with a network of cable cars in every direction, its visitors drawn above all by the winter sports complexes. La Plagne (*below*), is a new resort designed for experienced skiers who are looking for difficult slopes. By day people live on their skis, drifting from glaciers to alpine pastures, and in the evenings, seated by the fireside, they discuss the day's skiing. Émile Allais, the skiing champion, recognised the exceptional potential of the site and was one of the founders of the resort. The timber-clad buildings, designed to be unobtrusive, are highly functional; some are connected by heated corridors and the countless *pistes* run right up to the chalets.

Overleaf: **Mont Blanc, Haute-Savoie**
The gigantic peaks, ridges and precipices of the Mont Blanc *massif*, ranged one behind the other like breakers in a sea of rocks and stone, can evoke nothing but awe and astonishment. The Mer de Glace, its largest glacier, is 18 kilometres in length.

Vézelay, Yonne

Vézelay, which lies on the pilgrimage route to Santiago de
Compostela, between Burgundy and Morvan, was one of the most
famous shrines of Christendom in medieval times. Vézelay had been a
simple Benedictine foundation, but its fame grew because the relics of
Mary Magdalen were kept, or so it was believed, in the abbey. By the
early twelfth century it became necessary to extend the original
Merovingian church to contain those who came to worship, but
shortly after building work had started the nave caught fire and
burnt down, killing more than a thousand people trapped inside. The
work was soon under way again and by the middle of the century the
nave was completed, to which, in the thirteenth century the choir and
Romano-Gothic transept were added. These were times of glory for
Vézelay: St Bernard came to preach, and Philip Augustus and
Richard the Lionheart to carry the cross of the Second Crusade,
while St Louis came twice to pray at the altar. But at the end of the
thirteenth century, when relics of Mary Magdalen were discovered
elsewhere, at Saint-Maximin in Provence, doubts began to stir in the
souls of the pious, the pilgrims deserted Vézelay and the fairs and
markets which flourished in the wake of great pilgrim processions also
tailed away. Later, during the sixteenth-century religious wars,
Vézelay was sacked by Huguenots and at the time of the French
Revolution, part of the church was rased to the ground. It was only in
the nineteenth century that the abbey was restored to its former
glory, thanks entirely to Prosper Mérimée, who was at the time an
Inspector of Public Monuments. He passed the task of restoration to
Viollet-le-Duc, who, working from old documents, spent nineteen
years on the intricate and painstaking work of reconstituting the
church from the ruins. Although Viollet-le-Duc's restoration has
sometimes been severely criticised, it is only thanks to his efforts that
Vézelay retains its beauty, with splendid fragments of the original
abbey, and that the houses still climb in orderly procession to the foot
of the basilica of Sainte-Madelaine.

Sully, Saône-et-Loire

Medieval Burgundy, a monastic society dominated by the great abbey of Cluny, gave way in the sixteenth century to a society open to change, renewal and the artistic and intellectual influences of Renaissance Italy. The fairy-tale château of Sully (*left*) in the *département* of Saône-et-Loire captures that spirit perfectly in the harmony between the elegant proportions of the castle and its outbuildings and the gracious layout of the gardens and grounds. Jean de Saulx gave orders for the construction of the castle at the beginning of the sixteenth century and his son, the Marshal of Tavannes, carried on the work. The four perfectly proportioned wings are flanked by square towers, the façades are ornamented by pilasters and the castle's chapel nestles between two overhanging turrets. On the north side, a monumental staircase leads down to a terrace overlooking the moat.

57

Châteauneuf, Nièvre

Châteauneuf (*right*), a picturesque Burgundian medieval village in
the Val-de-Bargis has kept its strong outer walls, great round towers,
drawbridges and Gothic buildings, but the château now keeps watch
only over the vineyards of the rich Burgundian countryside.

Clos de Vougeot, Côte d'Or

The peaceful château of Clos de Vougeot (*below*), just south of Dijon,
was begun in the twelfth century, completed during the Renaissance
and restored in the nineteenth century. It seems to symbolise the
deep-rooted Burgundian appreciation of the pleasures of life.
Stendhal related the tale of a colonel in the Napoleonic army who
made his regiment present arms in honour of the castle and all it
represented, and since the last war the château has been owned by
the famous epicurean brotherhood of the Chevaliers du Tastevin.
Around five hundred guests gather here every year for the *disnée*, the
formal supper and highly colourful ceremony – based on the
divertissement in Molière's *Malade Imaginaire* – during which the Grand
Master and Grand Chamberlain, surrounded by dignitaries, formally
admit new *chevaliers* to the order.

Overleaf: **Tonnerre, Yonne**

The Church of Saint-Pierre in Tonnerre still presides over the small
town. In the sixteenth century a fire swept through the town and the
church was destroyed. Rebuilt on its high platform, the church has
reigned in tranquility over the rooftops, vines, fields and clear waters
of the river below ever since.

Semur-en-Auxois, Côte d'Or

Semur-en-Auxois (*right*), on the River Armençon, has a vigorous beauty. The Tower of the Orle d'Or and parapet walk around the ramparts are reminders that Semur was reputedly once an impregnable fortified town and the little houses, citadel and church are clustered in a ravine under a towering pink granite cliff. The church of Notre-Dame – its tapering spire, the height of the vaulting accentuated by the straightness of the nave and the portal crowned by an angel with open arms – gives an impression of flight towards the sky. On one of the little columns framing the portal, two carved snails remind us that Burgundy has long been a region of good living.

La Rochepot, Côte d'Or

The feudal château of La Rochepot (*below*) is one of the finest examples of architecture in Burgundy, and its setting captures all that is best in the local landscape. Colour and form are in perfect balance: the coloured roofs and soft brickwork of the castle set against the luxuriant green forest, the refined lines and robust elegance of the towers against the soft roundness of the dales.

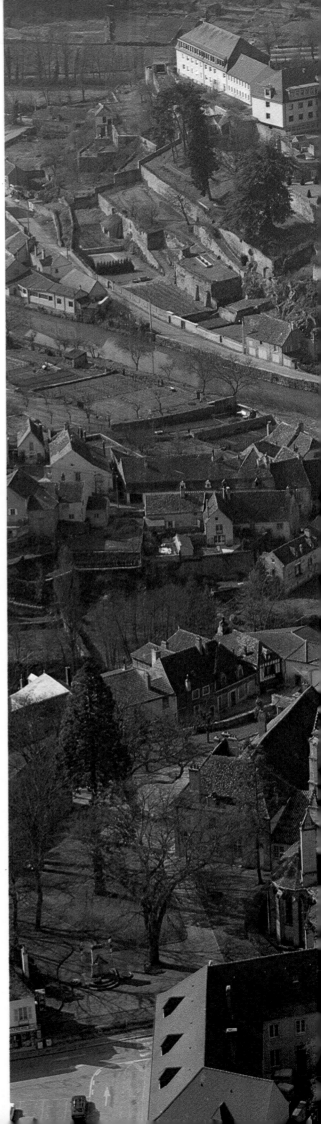

Tournus, Saône-et-Loire

Tournus (*above*), on the right bank of the Saône in the rolling Mâconnais countryside, is one of the oldest monastic centres in France, its harmonious beauty revealing little of the vicissitudes it has known. The original Merovingian abbey grew from sanctuaries erected on the tomb of St Valérien, a Christian from Asia Minor who met his martyrdom here in the second century. In the ninth century the arrival of monks who brought with them the relics of St Philibert led to rapid expansion, but in 937, the Magyars set fire to the abbey. Restored to its former state, it was abandoned some years later, but after the former prior had received orders to return and rebuild it, the work was completed. Pillaged and restored several times since then, it was only when the abbey became a parish church in the eighteenth century that its future was finally assured. It is now the heart of a charming town in the wine-growing area between Chalon and Mâcon. In the area around Tournus there are no fewer than two hundred examples of Romanesque architecture.

Arnay-le-Duc, Côte d'Or

The historical associations of Arnay-le-Duc (*right*) belong to military and political history. Here the forces of Henry of Navarre, the future Huguenot Henry IV, clashed swords with the troops of Mayenne in the very first of the many battles he was to fight. La Motte Forte, a massive round tower topped with a *machicoulis*, a parapet with narrow openings through which an attack could be repulsed from above, is now the sole remaining vestige of the important feudal château around which many battles raged during the sixteenth-century wars between the Catholics and the Huguenots. The château was captured, and recaptured, by both sides, but fortunately the town survived.

Fontenay, Côte d'Or

In a solitary valley in the Côte d'Or, to the north-east of Montbard,
stands the abbey of Fontenay. The austerity of the Cistercian rule is
echoed in the stark simplicity of architecture: the façade of the
twelfth-century abbey church, built at the time of St Bernard, the
founder of the order, is bare of all ornament. Only seven bays,
symbolising the sacraments, serve to accentuate the two buttresses.
The nave respects the same spirit of simplicity. The cloister abutting
the southern wall of the church (each gallery with eight bays defined
by buttresses), is equally severe architecturally and the gardens
surrounding the monastery are laid out in absolutely straight lines.
Conditions of life here were hard, for the Cistercian rule forbade the
monks to receive any tithes or land. Divine office occupied six or
seven hours of their daily routine; the rest of the time was spent
studying the scriptures and in manual labour. The monks were also
known for their cultivation of medicinal plants. Today, the abbey is
still a place of peace and contemplation and it has preserved the
majestic silence of the medieval centuries.

Overleaf: **Sarthe**
A golden cornfield between Chartres and Le Mans in the *département*
of Sarthe.

Vosges Mountains

In winter, snow sharpens the outlines of the blue horizons of the Vosges, enhancing the beauty and mystery of this land of legendary glory, once the haunt of wolves. To the south of the chain are the crystalline, granite Vosges: the swelling crests and rounded summits facing west towards Lorraine and the escarpments, bristling with spikes of rock, of the slope facing Alsace. From the air, the southern Vosges appear to be packed tightly one against the other, running in frozen waves to all points of the compass. Separated from them by the valley of the River Bruche, the northern Vosges take on more interesting shapes. High platforms lie on the summits, *corniches* project above gorges with rushing streams, and great slabs of rock pile up to form impressive overhangs. These are the mountains that have provided the marvellous, fine-grained red sandstone used to construct town walls, châteaus, churches and cathedrals throughout this region. With great foresight, the medieval abbeys prevented over-exploitation of the forests, so that today, centuries later, the pine trees, spruces and sycamores covering the densely shadowed slopes still play an important part in the local economy, as the basis of both the timber industry and tourism.

71

Riquewihr, Haut-Rhin and Minversheim, Bas-Rhin

Two aerial panoramas showing Alsace as it once was: the small town of Riquewihr (*left*) and the village of Minversheim (*below*), radiating out from its church. Visitors to Riquewihr, a wine-town known for its Riesling, see the town today just as it was in the sixteenth century. The château, built around 1539, has retained its mullioned windows, gables topped with deer antlers and winding staircase inside a turret. The Tower of Thieves, which was formerly a prison with a torture chamber and *oubliettes* – secret dungeons – now forms part of the remains of the town ramparts and communicates with the curious Court of the Jews, the old ghetto, by means of a narrow passage. Along the winding streets one finds beautiful, evocatively named old houses vying with each other in elegance and attention to detail. One displays galleries with wooden balustrades, another bay windows framed with twisted mouldings and elaborate carvings of stems, flowers and fruits, while nearly all the houses boast winding staircases, overhanging balconies, courtyards and wells.

Overleaf: **Sélestat, Bas-Rhin**

Lying on the left bank of the River Ill, Sélestat is a double city: on one side is the new town, with a variety of industries, and on the other the old town, with the magnificent Romanesque church of Sainte-Foy, built in red sandstone and granite. The other treasures of old Sélestat include the town arsenal, a gracious fourteenth-century building, the clock tower dating from the same period and the ramparts attributed to Vauban. A walkway along the parapets gives a superb view across the hills below the Vosges to Haut-Koenigsbourg castle.

Haut-Koenigsbourg, Bas-Rhin

Anchored on a rocky outcrop to the west of Sélestat, the imposing
château of Haut-Koenigsbourg (*right*) watches over the mountain
passes into the Rhine valley. Like a mighty sentinel, the fortress,
encircled by a triple outer wall, dominates the Alsace plain, and from
high on its ramparts there is an extraordinarily impressive view of
dark forests and lovely countryside stretching into the distance.
Already in existence in the twelfth century, when it belonged to the
lords of Sélestat, the Staufen, the medieval fortress was rebuilt three
centuries later but destroyed during the Thirty Years' War, and
remained an untouched ruin for over three centuries. In 1901 the
town of Sélestat, which had insufficient funds to undertake
conservation work, presented Haut-Koenigsbourg to Kaiser Wilhelm
II, who decided to restore, rather than simply preserve the castle, with
results that are still the subject of much debate. On the occasion of his
last visit in 1918, he had fixed on the ironwork of the fireplace the
famous inscription, 'That is not what I desired'.

Hunawihr, Haut-Rhin

Hunawihr (*below*), a charming wine-growing town, is also well-
defended; the belltower of its fortified church, encircled by six
bulwarks, is as massive and solid as the keep of a castle. Both Roman
Catholic and Protestant services are held in the church, which has
given its nave a rather distinctive appearance. But the charm of the
town derives from the typically Alsatian shape of its houses and the
slope of its roofs.

La Petite-Pierre, Bas-Rhin, and Ronchamp, Haut-Saône

La Petite-Pierre (*right*), a fortified village in the Lower Vosges dating from the end of the twelfth century, and the Chapel of Notre-Dame du Haut (*above*), at Ronchamp in the Haute-Saône, erected during the 1950s by Le Corbusier, provide two very different examples of the way in which buildings merge with the landscape. La Petite-Pierre occupies a dominant position above the heart of the wooded *massif* of the Lower Vosges; an area of the surrounding forest has been designated as a reserve for larger gamebirds and also offers shelter to deer. The castle fortress dates from the end of the twelfth century and its church from the beginning of the fourteenth century, whilst the village also boasts a fine Renaissance house, fortifications designed by Vauban, a chapel and an historic underground reservoir. The more recent buildings also blend harmoniously into the landscape through the use of local building materials and respect for traditional methods.

Le Corbusier's chapel at Ronchamp achieves an inspired resolution of austerity, severity of line and restrained use of materials. Built on the site of an ancient hilltop sanctuary destroyed in 1944, the curved, steeply pitched walls, covered with very plain rendering, support the double hull of the reinforced concrete roof. An external altar, under a large canopy, allows Mass to be celebrated with the priest facing the congregation assembled on the hillside. A striking demonstration of the architectural principles of its innovative designer, the building both adapts itself to the site and stands apart from it.

Montmédy, Meuse

Montmédy, a large market town in the peaceful valley of the River Chiers, near the Ardennes, is in reality two quite separate towns: the lower is stretched out by the side of the river, while the upper is isolated on a rocky spur. Fortified during the Renaissance, it has kept its drawbridges and ramparts practically intact. The history of La Ville Haute, situated right in the middle of an invasion route, is enmeshed with chaotic upheavals of war and politics. During the Middle Ages it was the capital of the *comté* of Chiny, in the middle of the fifteenth century it passed into the power of the Dukes of Burgundy and, shortly afterwards, the Hapsburgs of Austria became its masters. Then, in the sixteenth century it came under the rule of the King of Spain before finally, in 1659, under Louis xiv, it became French territory. In our own century the town has once again been a battlefield, this time during the fierce fighting which took place between the Meuse, the Ardennes and Argonne in 1914; the soldiers of the garrison here were massacred during a desperate attempt to reach the French lines after they had been completely surrounded by the enemy.

Charleville, Ardennes

The rigidly geometrical architecture of Charleville (*above*), and Sedan (*right*), the regional capitals of the Meuse valley, convey a sense of order, opulence and prudent conservatism. Charleville, built in 1608 on a bend of the River Meuse by order of Charles of Gonzaga, Duke of Nevers and Mantua and Governor of Champagne, was fortified 'rather by way of ornament than to make it a fortified town', and it has particularly lovely monuments. The finest feature is the rectangular *place*, a twin to the Place des Vosges in Paris, which is surrounded by prosperous brick or stone houses with high slate roofs and elegant, arcaded galleries. On the edge of the river lie a museum and quay named after Arthur Rimbaud, who lived and wrote *Le Bateau ivre* here.

Sedan, Ardennes

Sedan is a showcase of military architecture, laid out in an irreproachably well-ordered pattern around Château Bas, the largest fortress in Europe. Built on a rock, it towers over the city and the River Meuse beneath. The design and construction of the fortress, dating from the fifteenth century with ramparts linked by later walls made of vast irregular stones, foreshadows the work of Vauban.

Overleaf: **Ardennes**

The hilly landscape of the Ardennes, north of Verdun, its harshness softened by centuries of erosion, a thick blanket of gloomy forest and a dramatic purple sky. The forests here remained unchanged for many centuries.

Flandre and Artois

Flandre and Artois, the flat country stretching out to meet the North Sea. This land has been the chosen route for some of the greatest invasions in history and the theatre of some of the bloodiest battles ever fought in Europe. The North contains two, even three, quite different regions: the collieries and mining villages of the 'Black Country', the chessboard of open fields stretching from there to the coast, and finally, the long, sandy beaches of the North Sea. Many people pass quickly through the region without pausing to look at the countryside, but nobody could fail to recognise its gentle beauty. From the sky the countryside has the tones of a watercolour, soft yellows alternating with fresh greens and delicate pinks. The land is rich and it is worked hard; fields of wheat and beet, crossed by the dark lines of little hedges, stretch around the farmhouses, solid and four-square on their foundations, which remain isolated behind screens of trees (*left*, at Watten, north of Saint-Omer). The areas of marshland (*below*) now, as in the past, are continually cleared, drained and cultivated.

Overleaf: **Saint-Omer, Pas-de-Calais**
It was the Benedictine monks of Saint-Omer who first drained and canalised the famous *watergangs*, the marshes surrounding the abbey town, in the Middle Ages. The local people continued the work and so created a rich, peaceful countryside of canals, fields and little woods.

Rocroi, Ardennes
The town of Rocroi, known for the Duke of Condé's great victory over the Spanish here in 1643, is situated on a plateau in the Ardennes. Its pale-coloured houses, roofed with slate, run along streets laid out like a spider's web; eight short, perfectly straight roads radiate out to the bulky, irregular ramparts from the huge central square. Outside the walls the roads snake across the lonely plateau once filled by the smoke of the canons and the sounds of battle.

Étretat, Seine-Maritime

The spectacular natural architecture of the Étretat (*right*) on the
Seine estuary in the Pays de Caux, was formed by the indefatigable
pounding of the sea against the limestone cliffs at high tide. All along
the Pays de Caux white cliffs, topped by rich green pastures and
gashed by small, dry valleys, rear up out of the waves. The
monumental arches here, the Porte d'Aval and Manneporte, were
made famous by Maupassant and the Impressionist painters.

Deauville, Calvados

Deauville (*above*), in the pleasant, green Pays d'Auge, is the most
famous of the many resorts in Normandy. First made fashionable as
an elegant resort by the Duke of Morny in the nineteenth century,
the villas, built in the inimitable style peculiar to Normandy, now
crowd alongside grand hotels and the casino, and the world famous
promenade, the *planches*, runs for three kilometres along the beach. A
racecourse, a golf course and the marina of Port-Deauville complete
the amenities. In the summer the *planches* are crowded with people
out for a stroll and in the autumn smart society finishes the season
here at the fashionable film festival, but by the end of the year only
5,000 residents remain to enjoy the peace and quiet of winter.

Mont-Saint-Michel, Manche

Mont-Saint-Michel, considered by some people to be Breton and by others to be Norman, originally served as a place of worship to unknown gods. According to local myth it was converted to Christian use by St Auber, Bishop of Avranches, on the orders of St Michael, but remained no more than a sanctuary until the beginning of the eighth century. Then the Benedictines founded the abbey and slowly the Carolingian, Romanesque and Gothic additions made between the tenth and sixteenth centuries combined to form the extraordinary fairy-tale abbey we know today. Crowning it all is the spire, built at the end of the nineteenth century when the island could still be reached only at low tide. It was in our own century that a causeway was built, linking Mont-Saint-Michel with the mainland. Underground, built into the rock, lie a series of chapels and chambers, among them Notre-Dame sous terre (Our Lady below ground), Notre-Dame des Trente Cierges (Our Lady of the Thirty Tapers), the Crypt of the Great Columns and the Knights' Hall. These support the thirteenth-century cloister and monastic buildings and the fifteenth-century abbey house. Recently the French government has taken steps to preserve Mont-Saint-Michel from the threat posed by the gradual silting up of the bay but it will never regain the silence that reigned before its invasion by hordes of tourists.

Saint-Malo, Ille-et-Vilaine

The atmosphere of the town of Saint-Malo remains a curious blend of adventure and sobriety, imagination and orderliness. Sited on a small granite island on the estuary of the River Rance, the solidity of the Ville Close, the walled town, stands out against the liquid green of the surrounding water and gives the impression of a town afloat. At one time the town was linked to the mainland only by a narrow isthmus, but causeways – with such evocative names as the chaussée des Corsaires – were later built, giving easier access to the newer parts of town on the mainland. Everything about the old town, from its granite ramparts and gates to its grand houses and handsome courtyards, tells the tale of the *grande course*, the days of piracy and privateering, when the sailors of Saint-Malo fired their broadsides against the ships of the Dutch, English and Spanish. To the north-west of the old town are a beach, hotels, a casino and a conference centre while to the south-east lie a marina, the commercial port and the fishing port, where old men with sailor's caps watch the ships through binoculars. Despite heavy bombardment during the Second World War, splendid houses, with stout walls and solid studded wooden doors, stand as reminders of corsair wealth and bygone glories. The château – now the *hôtel de ville* – constructed in the fifteenth century, is impressive, reinforced by bulwarks and flanked by four massive towers. One of these, built in 1475 by Duke Francis II, is nicknamed 'the General'; the other, added by his daughter, the Duchess Anne, is known as 'Quiquengrogne' from its insolent motto, 'Whosoever makes complaint, let him do so, for such is my right good pleasure.'

Saint-Servan-Sur-Mer, Ille-et-Vilaine

On the rocky Corniche d'Aleth of Saint-Servan (*right*), caravans now park in the City Fort, built in the eighteenth century and modernised and used by German forces in the last war. Behind, the fourteenth-century Solidor Tower, once a prison and now a maritime museum, looks down the Rance estuary towards the dam constructed to supply a tidal power station and which connects Saint-Malo and Saint-Servan to Dinard on the opposite bank.

This is an important area for sailing, windsurfing and all water-sports. The river is navigable by sailing boat as far as Dinan, a lovely old town with pale-coloured granite houses and high walls, and by boat one can reach the islands: Chausey and Bréhat, or, closer in, Harbour and Cézembre, which, despite their precipitous rocks, high waves and strong currents, are a paradise for fishermen searching for shrimps, crabs and other shellfish.

Dinard, Ille-et-Vilaine

The old town of Dinard, clinging to the cliff which dominates the Rance estuary, looks out over the shops and gardens of the new town centre. The fine houses of the old town include the Black Prince's manor house, which dates from the fifteenth century. To the north, looking out on to the open sea, lies the summer resort. The Vicomté, an old *domaine* now divided into separate plots of land, has become its residential annexe, with rows of prosperous looking villas set in gardens full of hortensia in shades of pink and blue. Here we find fig trees, palms, monkey-puzzles, myrtles and camelias flourishing in the shelter of the estuary and the even, oceanic climate, made still milder by the nearby Gulf Stream. Of the three main beaches, the Prieuré, the longest and flattest, runs between the old town and the Vicomté; the second, L'Écluse, lies between the headlands of Malouine and Moulinet and is flanked by a dyke with a promenade for pedestrians, while the third, Saint-Énogat, is a series of sandy strands with rocks that are uncovered at low tide. Finally, there is the Clair de Lune promenade, which runs from the slipway of Bec de la vallée to Prieuré beach.

Fort de la Latte, Côtes-du-Nord
From afar the Fort de la Latte, near Cape Fréhel, in Brittany, merges
with the tangled mass of granite on which it is built. Behind the rocky
promontory jutting out into the waves like the bows of a ship extends
a flattened, windswept heathland, and all around stretches the sea,
dark emerald or pale turquoise according to the weather. From high
on the keep one can look out over the bays of La Frênaye and Saint-
Malo, and the savage cliffs of the cove of Sévigné. In the Middle Ages
the fort, then the château of Roche-Guyon, belonged to the *seigneurs*
of Matignon. They built the high walls, towers and drawbridges
crossing the fissures in the cliff face, and they lived there in isolation,
keeping guard against invasion from the sea and attacks from the
land. Although the fort was restored by order of Louis XIV, it remains
entirely medieval in both architectural style and mood.

La Trinité-sur-Mer, Morbihan

At La Trinité-sur-Mer (*right*) and Concarneau (*above*), in southern Brittany, life follows the rhythm of the tide, and the day is measured by the departure and return of the fishing boats. At La Trinité-sur-Mer, built on a wide river estuary, the harbour is packed with barges, trawlers and pleasure boats tied up along narrow jetties, while the nearby coastline is dotted with beacons, lighthouses and oyster-beds. Only a few kilometres inland are the menhirs of Carnac and the megalithic monuments of Locmariaquer, the splendid relics of the mysterious world of the Druids.

Concarneau, Finistère

Concarneau is one of the liveliest and most colourful of the Breton ports. The houses, with blue slate roofs, crowd together along the alleyways. In the evening, the red, green and brown boats lie at anchor as tons of fish, caught off Scotland and Ireland and in tropical waters, are unloaded for sale by auction. The blue nets are spread out on the jetties to dry, while the fishermen, using their words sparingly, call out to one another in loud voices. Like Saint-Malo, Concarneau has a walled town, with medieval and Renaissance fortifications that were later added to by Vauban, and it now also has a sea-side resort by the white sands of the Baie de la Forêt.

Chambord, Loir-et-Cher

Everything about the château of Chambord, which the Emperor Charles V called 'a summary of human industry', is superb. Immense and elegant, it was built by Francis I as a splendid hunting lodge and it is thought that Leonardo da Vinci was responsible for some parts of the original design. The château itself has 440 rooms, while 32 kilometres of walls enclose the formal gardens and enormous area of natural parkland. Even the architectural detail of Chambord is magnificent: the famous staircase with its double ramp, designed to allow riders to go up to the apartments without dismounting, the dormer windows, the lanterns and sumptuously decorated fireplaces. Francis I even considered diverting the course of the River Loire so that his hunting lodge might have a mirror worthy of its magnificence, but royal impoverishment prevented his ambitious plan and the more modest River Cosson flows past the château instead. Louis XIV loved to stay at Chambord and the first performance of the *Bourgeois Gentilhomme* was given here. The 'magic château', as Alfred de Vigny described it, more recently witnessed the first historical *son et lumière*, devised to recount the story of Chambord to visitors over twenty years ago.

Chinon, Indre-et-Loire

The high walls which once enclosed Chinon (*right*), on the banks of the River Vienne, have now crumbled and its château, a twelfth-century fortress perched high on an escarpment, is no more than a shell, but the town has still retained its history and medieval character. Joan of Arc came here to beg Charles VII to provide her with troops who would 'drive the English out of France' and Rabelais was born not far away. The fifteenth-century houses with their stone gables, turrets, carved doors and mullioned windows, are full of atmosphere.

Langeais, Indre-et-Loire

The middle course of the River Loire describes a bend to the south of the Paris basin. Here the river stretches out as it flows placidly to the Atlantic, its waters peaceful and sparkling. Langeais (*below*), like many towns and châteaus of the Loire valley, appears poised between the water, the land and the sky; the gentle blues, greys and greens of the landscape merge around its long narrow bridge, which seems almost to be suspended above the water.

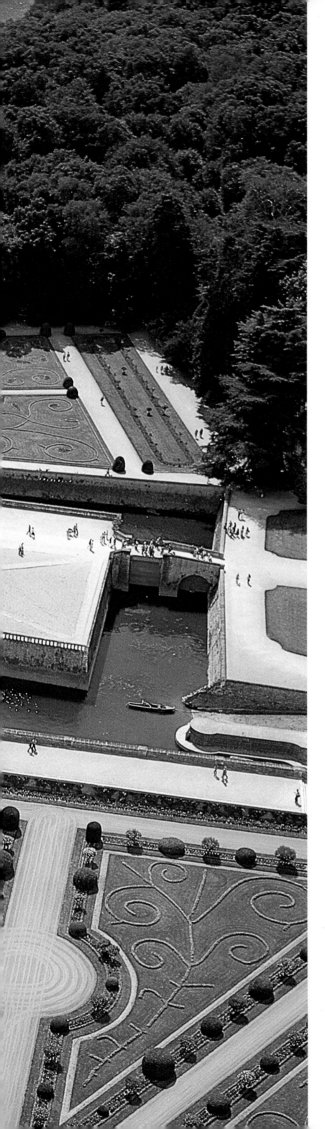

Chenonceaux, Indre-et-Loire

Chenonceaux (*left*), built on a series of arches across the River Cher, is often known at the 'château of six women'. The first of its six redoubtable chatelaines, Catherine Brissonet, oversaw the main building work at the beginning of the sixteenth century; the second, the beautiful Diane de Poitiers, laid out the garden and ordered the construction of the bridge linking the château to the far bank of the river; and the third, Catherine de Médici, had the park landscaped and the double gallery built on to the bridge. Chenonceaux became a refuge of mourning when Louise Vandémont de Lorraine retired here after the assassination of her husband, Henry III, and in the eighteenth century Jean-Jacques Rousseau stayed here as a guest of Madame Dupin while he was writing *Emile*. The sixth chatelaine, Madame Pelouze, made the restoration of Chenonceaux her life's work.

Azay-le-Rideau, Indre-et-Loire

Azay-le-Rideau (*below*), on the River Indre, is less spacious than Chenonceaux, but it has infinite charm. Dating from the early Renaissance, when castles were no longer primarily defensive, the traditional feudal fortifications became elegant architectural features with no real purpose other than the enhancement of the castle. The towers are here no more than turrets; the *machicoulis*, parapets which might once have been used to drop stones or boiling lead on to the heads of the invaders below, are purely ornamental, and the moats are harmless mirrors of water. Inside the château are superb sixteenth and seventeenth-century tapestries and furniture.

Ussé, Indre-et-Loire; Fontevraud, Maine-et-Loire; Luynes, Indre-et-Loire; Blois, Loir-et-Cher and Amboise, Indre-et-Loire
Five scenes from the Pays du Loire; Ussé (*opposite*), with its white stone, quaint roofs, belfries and dormer windows, said to be the castle of Perrault's Sleeping Beauty; Fontevraud (*above left*), a magnificent abbey dating from the eleventh century, which remains the largest intact group of monastic buildings in France;

Blois (*above right*), dubbed 'the Versailles of the Renaissance'; Luynes (*below right*), dominated by a feudal château with cellars hollowed deep into the bare rock; and, finally, Amboise (*below left*), where Charles VIII wanted to create an earthly paradise of Italian gardens and Leonardo da Vinci lived during the reign of Francis I. Today only the King's lodge remains to bear witness to the splendour of the original tapestries at Amboise.

La Rochelle and Fouras, Charente-Maritime

La Rochelle (*left*), the lovely capital of Aunis, and Fouras, a little town near the mouth of the River Charente, have the same mild weather and lush green countryside. Both also have fortified defences: although the architecture of La Rochelle is more impressive with ramparts and towers, little medieval houses and noble seventeenth and eighteenth-century mansions, secret passages and arcades. In the seventeenth century the town was a Protestant stronghold and twenty-five thousand inhabitants starved to death during the blockade led by Cardinal Richelieu. Now, however, the overwhelming impression is only of beauty and harmony.

In the fifteenth century, the keep at Fouras guarded the entrance to the River Charente. In summer the long swell of the Atlantic meets golden cornfields (*above*), and, where one gives way to the other, oyster-beds stand neatly lined up along the white sand beach.

Marennes and La Cayenne, Charente-Maritime

In the area around Marennes and La Cayenne in the southern
Charente-Maritime lies an extraordinary lake-city, its waterways
continually busy with flat-bottomed boats and slender dories. Here
four thousand hectares of the Seudre estuary have been turned over
to oyster cultivation. The seed-oysters, deposited on trays of tiles
treated with lime or on strips of slate, grow into young oysters in the
open sea, then after eight to ten months they are transferred to basins.
Here they are left for another year, until they reach adolescence,
before being moved again to *claires*, large reservoirs built in disused
salt marshes, where the final refining and fattening takes place.
Among the sea of fields are anchored little villages like L'Éguille,
Mornac-sur-Seudre, Nieulle-sur-Seudre or Chaillevette, were the sole
activity is oyster breeding.

Pointe du Chapus, Charente-Maritime
During the Middle Ages, the *gats*, or salt marshes of the west coast, were a prosperous area, since salt was then as valuable as gold. Brouage, one of the most beautiful ports in France, was the largest centre of the trade in Europe, and the rest of the coast, including Oléron, the lovely Île de Ré, Marennes and Le Chapus , drew its wealth from the marshes in the same way. In the eighteenth century, Brouage still rivalled La Rochelle as a commercial centre, but as the marshes began to silt up and the climate became unhealthy, it slowly declined and became an abandoned town. The marshes remained and while polders were made away from the coast, towards the sea the cultivation of oysters was established.

Quatre Vaux and Parc d'Isigny, Charente-Maritime
The *claires* of the Marennes basin, like those at Quatre Vaux (*left*)
and Parc d'Isigny (*below*), annually produce 40,000 tonnes of oysters.
It is hard and worrying work: the oyster beds must be constantly
watched for disease or pollution, which can destroy the oysters in a
matter of days. The importance of the oyster trade in the local
economy – this region is responsible for half the total French national
production – is reflected by the existence of specialist museums at
Marennes, Fort Louvois, Étaules, and La Tremblade, and the
general interest in the methods of cultivation is such that there are
now regular visits to the oyster-beds from the ports of Le Chapus,
Bourcefranc, Marennes or Château d'Oléron.

Dune du Pilat, Gironde

The sheltered basin of the River Arcachon lies in the only large channel cutting the shoreline of the Côte d'Argent. At low tide both shelves of the seabed are exposed but at high tide part of the shoals remain visible thanks to the dykes around the Audenge and Teich reservoirs. Inland stand the resin-perfumed forests of the Landes, dotted with lakes, many of which connect with the sea. At the southern end of the basin is Pilat-Plage, which has the highest sand dune in Europe, the Pilat (*above*). This dazzling ridge of sand has actually grown slightly over the last century, despite the winds which whip across it. A footbridge and staircase lead to the top, and from here there is a magnificent view: on one side the forest, on the other the endlessly frothing and churning waves. There are two ways to come down the mountain, either by staircase or, for the more daring, on skis.

Pyrenees

The hinterland of the Atlantic Pyrenees (*left*) lies in steps against the skyline, valleys and prairies alternating with the gentle foothills and rougher peaks of the mountains. Here villages with unpronounceable Basque names lie along high winding roads and the snows melt into rushing torrents. On the French side of the border, the mountains climb in the central area to over 3,000 metres. Travelling is difficult, particularly from north to south, and the arterial routes from Paris to Barcelona and Bordeaux to Madrid run through Hendaye and Corbière to avoid the mountains.

Saint-Jean-de-Luz and Biarritz, Pyrénées-Atlantiques

Descending from the mountain to the coast, one comes first to Hendaye, then to Saint-Jean-de-Luz and Biarritz. Saint-Jean-de-Luz (*below*) has a long beach curving around the end of a peaceful bay and a magnificent Baroque church, Saint-Jean-Baptiste, where Louis XIV married Maria-Theresa of Spain. The main activity of the picturesque port is tuna fishing. Biarritz (*bottom*), originally a whaling port, was first made popular as a resort by the Empress Eugénie during the Second Empire, and it has remained one of the most sophisticated and famous of French seaside towns.

Bonifacio, Corsica

Corsica, a mountain fortress and magnificent remnant of the ancient Tyrrhenian continent, lies between the Côte d'Azur and the Tuscan coast. Over the centuries the coastal towns were fortified and high defensive walls erected, either by townspeople in need of protection against marauders' incursions or by conquerors wanting to consolidate new possessions. Bonifacio (*right*), perched on a limestone promontory on the southern Corsican coast, always had formidable natural defences, but they were completed in the Middle Ages by Bonifacio, a Tuscan noble, who erected an outer wall which is still perfect today. According to *The Odyssey*, Ulysses visited the town during his long journeying. The towns are set against a wild and beautiful coastline, with inlets and gulfs carved out of red porphyry and sparkling white limestone. Above the clear waters hang the combined scents of aloes, juniper, cistus, lavender, myrtle, mastic and eucalyptus.

La Pietra, Corsica

La Pietra, five rocky islets standing off the Île-Rousse, offers the most splendid of Mediterranean panoramas. Its old tower is now no more than an abandoned sentinel, but the lighthouse continues to guide boats away from the rocks. The Île-Rousse itself is today connected to the shore by a jetty, but it still jealously preserves its own identity as a separate island. Taking its name from its russet-coloured soil, with a superb beach of pale sand that attracts many tourists, it is known by the Corsicans as the 'oil and wheat country'. Palm trees, aloes and prickly pears grow alongside the wheat and the orange groves, and citrus fruit is shipped from the ports of Calvi and Île-Rousse.

Collioure, Pyrénées-Orientales
Collioure in the eastern Pyrenees was once called Cauco Illiberis
and is still Catalan in character. A fortified town, fishing port and
gentle seaside town rolled into one, it has a dramatic backdrop of
high red and green escarpments. Visitors delight in the town's
defensive walls, the old royal château and the château of the
Knights Templar, built between the thirteenth and fourteenth
centuries, while the old quarter of the Maura evokes the mood of
North African casbahs. At the beginning of this century Matisse,
Derain, Dufy and Juan Gris fell in love with Collioure and by the
end of the last war it was named an 'artist's town'.

Overleaf: **Carcassonne, Aude**
On the other side of the Corbières in the Aude, is a superb
miniature medieval world in perfect order even after five hundred
years. It is said to have been the greatest fortified city in medieval
Europe and, thanks to the restoration work done by Viollet-le-Duc
at the end of the last century, nothing is missing: the double outer
wall, drawbridges, moats, barbicans and the château are still
completely intact.

Puy Pariou, Puy-de-Dôme
To the west of Clermont-Ferrand are the *puys* of the Auvergne,
extinct volcanic cones stretched out like a chain of small mountains
against a unique landscape in shades of dark blue, grey and black.
Some of the volcanos have shimmering lakes in their craters and
plants and trees growing on their outer slopes; others, like the Puy
Pariou (*right*) – named after the Auvergnat word *pertiou* meaning a
hole – still have lava cliffs and raw craters which seem ready to spit
fire and flames. At the foot of the volcanos are deep undulating
valleys with Romanesque abbeys sculpted from the black lava and
grey stone in a remarkable pure architectural style. In the
seventeenth century, high-class courtesans who wanted to recover
from the excesses of life at Versailles began to come to this area to
benefit from the thermal springs, and tourism is still an important
source of income today.

Overleaf: **Versailles, Yvelines**
Louis XIV assembled the most brilliant talents to build and decorate
his palace: Le Vau and Hardouin-Mansart as architects, Vauban to
design the hydraulic system, Le Nôtre to lay out the gardens, Le Brun
to decorate the splendid state rooms and private apartments and
Mignard to carry out a series of paintings. The resulting perfect
proportions, grandiose scale and impressive façade gave the Sun
King his desired magnificence.

Rambouillet, Yvelines

Four French kings – Françis I, Louis XV, Louis XVI and Charles X – slept under the high grey roofs of Rambouillet and the Republic's most distinguished visitors have always been received here. The unusual pentagonal layout of the château comes from the medieval fortress that originally occupied the site, but its architecture is a compendium of style and taste from the Renaissance to the nineteenth century. The main body of buildings, dating from the seventeenth and eighteenth centuries, particularly the latter, are built on to the fifteenth-century great tower, but a third wing was destroyed in the early nineteenth century at Napoleon's orders. In the grounds the eighteenth-century English garden counterbalances the rather rigid formality of the French garden, farm and Queen's dairy, which date from the time of Louis XVI.

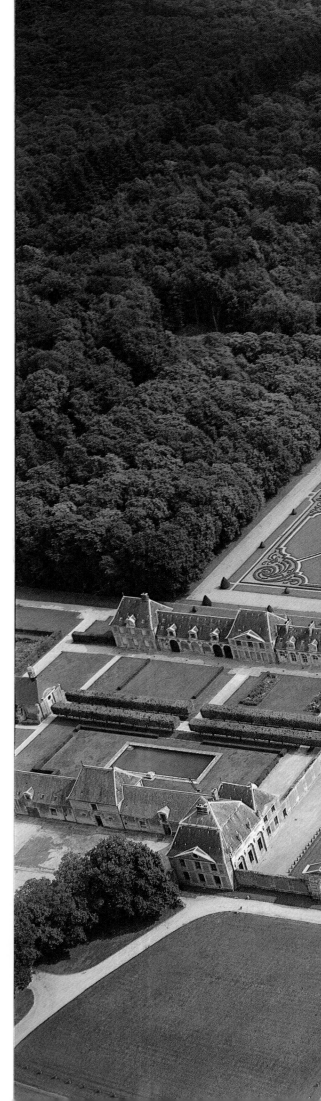

Vaux-le-Vicomte, Seine-et-Marne

The enchanting château of Vaux-le-Vicomte (*right*) is a perfect
example of the seventeenth-century Louis XIV style. Built by
Fouquet, the king's chancellor and one of his most powerful ministers,
it is said to have inspired Louis XIV – in large part from jealousy – to
build Versailles, which follows the same style on a much grander
scale. Le Vau was the architect, Le Brun was responsible for the
design of the interiors and La Nôtre for the design of the gardens and
parkland.

Fontainebleau, Seine-et-Marne

Travelling from Vaux-le-Vicomte to Fontainebleau (*below*) is a
journey back to the Renaissance. Francis I ordered a mason, Gilles le
Breton, to refashion the walls of the old defensive castle here along
Renaissance lines: the interior esplanade became the main courtyard,
pilasters reminiscent of Chambord (*see page 107*) were added to the
façades and later a peristyle and portico were added. In the king's
eyes, Fontainebleau was to be not simply a royal hunting lodge but
also the setting for an art collection intended to rival those of the
great Italian palaces, and the interior was therefore magnificently
decorated by Rosso and Primatriccio. The palace has subsequently
been modified, enlarged and its contents rearranged by successive
French monarchs, and the town has grown around it, but the famous
forest where the royal hunts took place remains as peaceful as ever.

Chantilly, Oise

The château of Chantilly (*left*), one of a chain surrounding the Île-de-France, was rebuilt in the mid-nineteenth century by the Duke of Aumale. Once a Gallo-Roman stronghold, then a Capetian fortress and afterwards a château with both defensive and Renaissance features, it was rebuilt along classical lines, but by the time of the Revolution there remained only the lodge built for the master of the royal hunt at the end of the sixteenth century. The Duke of Aumale's château appears rather too new, but it houses some very fine works of art, and the park, with its terraces and expanses of water, is full of charm.

Pierrefonds, Oise

In the nearby forest of Compiègne stands another restored château, Pierrefonds (*above*). The restoration was the work of Viollet-le-Duc, who, initially intended to restore the keep only, and to preserve the picturesque ruins around it. But once the work was under way, he rebuilt all the towers and façades dismantled under Louis XIII along the lines of his own invention, and, in so doing created a great romantic monument on a medieval theme.

Overleaf : **Sarthe**
A ploughed field in the *département* of Sarthe.

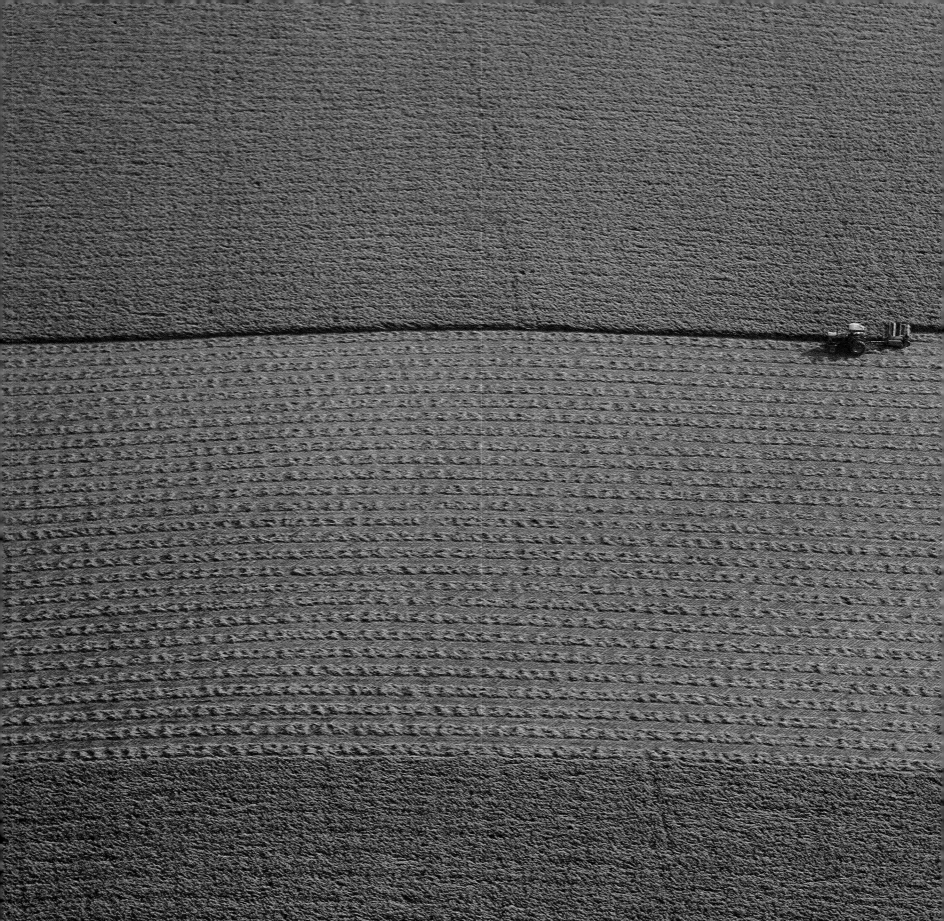

Chartres, Eure-et-Loire
Built in an extraordinary burst of religious fervour between the
twelfth and thirteenth centuries, Chartres cathedral has lost
nothing of its original purity or soaring quality over the centuries.
The superb belltowers point high above the wheatfields of the
Beauce. 'The most solid spike that was ever thrust into the air',
wrote the poet Charles Péguy of the marvellous Romanesque
belltower. The slender, graceful pillar supporting the nave is an
architectural marvel, while the stained glass windows, in
particular the rose window of the royal portal, show perfect
aesthetic judgement. Finally, the sculpture, on a theme which is
almost unique in the history of art – Adam in the mind of God
before creation – is of an infinite richness and variety.

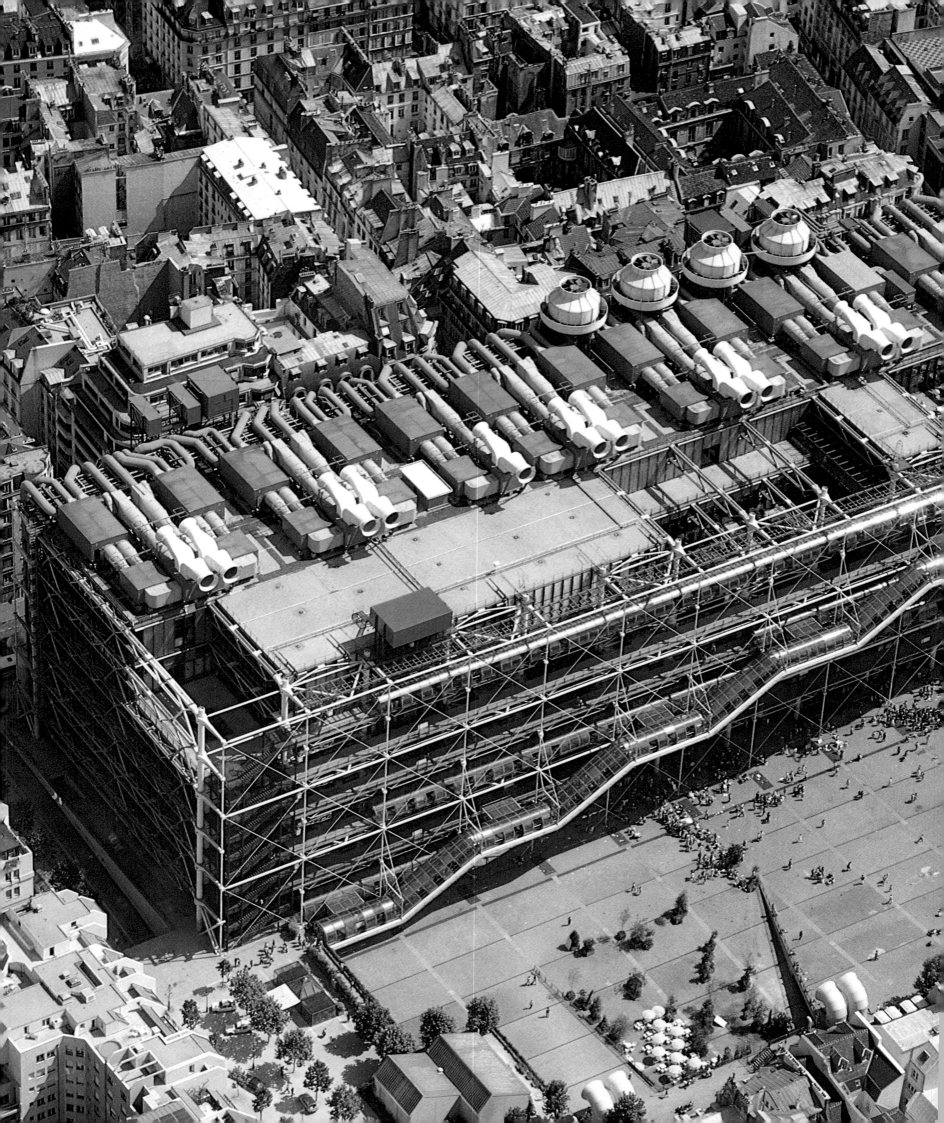

Beaubourg, Paris

The Georges Pompidou National Centre of Art and Culture,
usually known simply as the Beaubourg was conceived by Georges
Pompidou as an immense cultural complex to mark the seven
years of his presidency. The three architects – two Italians, Piano
and Franchini, and an Englishman, Rogers – produced a powerful
and innovatory design, which exposed the bare bones and
engineering of the building and excluded any ornamentation, and
the building was opened to the public in 1977. Its detractors
nicknamed it 'the oil refinery' and labelled it an outrage to art, but
others considered it a work of genius. Now, nearly a decade after it
opened, most Parisians agree that the building blends perfectly
with its background, and there can be no doubt that it has become
one of the major attractions of the city, with a marvellous art
collection, library and calender of cultural events, and a perpetual
carnival atmosphere in the adjacent square. Quite simply, one
cannot now imagine Paris without the Beaubourg.

Île de la Cité, Les Invalides and Arc de Triomphe, Paris

On the Île de la Cité (*right*), the birthplace of the capital, stands the serene church of Notre-Dame, built at the beginning of the thirteenth century by Maurice de Sully. Les Invalides (*below*), on the left bank, was created by Louis XIV to take in wounded soldiers, and its strictly ordered layout, majestic dome and façade are typical of the architecture he favoured to symbolise his power. Les Invalides is associated also with Napoleon, whose ashes have lain here since 1840, but his imperial spirit is more fittingly commemorated by the Arc de Triomphe (*bottom*) and the avenues radiating out from it, each of which – with the exception of the Champs-Élysées – bears the name of an illustrious general or Napoleonic victory.

Overleaf: **Eiffel Tower, Paris**

The Eiffel Tower, designed as a monument to industrial achievement for the Exposition universelle of 1889, was criticised on aesthetic grounds when it was first erected, but it is now seen simply as the symbol of the city spread at its feet.

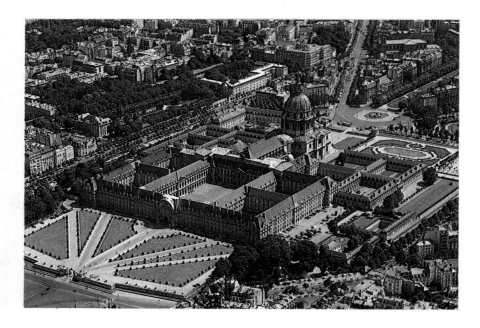

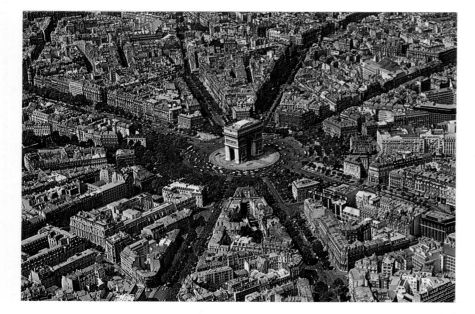

INDEX OF PLATES

The photographs are by Daniel Philippe with the exception of the following, which are reproduced by permission of l'agence Explorer: pages 105, 124, 125 bottom, 126, 127, 128–9, 143, 148–9, 150, 151, 152–3.